A New Hat for Hen

Barbara N. Herbert

Illustrated by Graeme Viljoen

Hen is going shopping.
She wants to buy a new hat.

Hen finds a piece of paper.
She cannot read.

Can you read this paper for
me? Hen asks Monkey.
No. I cannot read, Monkey says.

Can you read this paper for me? Hen asks Rabbit.
No. I cannot read, Rabbit says.

Hen meets Turtle.
Can you read this paper for
me? she asks Turtle.

Turtle can read.
But his eyes are very bad.
He says, I cannot see the words.

Hen is sad.
She wants to read the paper.
What can I do? she asks.

Turtle says, You must learn to read.
You must buy an alphabet book.

Hen buys an alphabet book.
Now she has no money to buy
a new hat.

Hen learns the letters of the
alphabet.
Then she learns to read words.

Hen finds the paper again.
She can read it now.

It is a lucky number!
Hen wins a lot of money.

Hen goes to the hat shop.
She buys a new hat.

And she buys a pair of glasses
for Turtle.

Activity

Which animals in the story can read?